C000084406

Tr
the Countryside

Also from the Emma Press

Poetry anthologies

Poetry anthologies for children

The Emma Press Picks

Poetry pamphlets

True Tales of the Countryside

By Deborah Alma

With an introduction
by Helen Ivory

THE EMMA PRESS

for Jim, with love

THE EMMA PRESS

First published in Great Britain in 2015
by the Emma Press Ltd

Poems copyright © Deborah Alma 2015
Introduction copyright © Helen Ivory 2015

ISBN 978-1-910139-26-4

A CIP catalogue record of this book
is available from the British Library.

Printed and bound in Great Britain
by Letterworks Ltd, Reading.

theemmapress.com
queries@theemmapress.com

Introduction

A collection that begins *I put a pen in my cunt once* could only have been written by a woman. My thoughts are drawn inevitably towards Eve Ensler's *The Vagina Monologues*, and then to Germaine Greer's work on women reclaiming "the c-word", an ancient word with various derivations, none of them tabooed.

Greer said in a BBC series about language: 'I love the idea that this word is still so sacred you can use it like a torpedo [...] It's a word of immense power – to be used sparingly.' And this is what Deborah Alma does. She only uses it once, but the metaphor of the writer's cunt taking up a pen and writing these poems out of sheer loneliness means that each one of these poems could be read as a vagina monologue, so to speak.

So what do we have here? *True Tales of the Countryside* is about the earthiness, the sexiness and the resourcefulness of being a woman. It is about how a woman rediscovers herself after a marriage and how she remakes her home.

These are poems of lived experience threaded through with folksongs and tales from the oral tradition. Alma brings together supermarkets and wolves with 'what big teeth' for equal consideration and sits tight on a box holding love letters in 'On Sleeping Alone', emphasising that she is a real woman, not part of a story: 'Pandora was not heavy on her hips like me not grounded by her own strong living days and nights... I am drawn instead to my own songs... love letters to myself...'

All of these poems are vital: they are scented with patchouli, mother's milk, sheep-bitten grass and sex; they are scuffing up the heels of their reddest shoes; they are letters of love, penned in sour cream.

Helen Ivory
September 2015

Contents

I put a pen in my cunt once

just to play with myself
when I was at a loose end
when we were in one of those times
lying in straight lines in the dark
not touching

long hands stroke
my words to sour cream
this is what it wrote

New House

On the first warm days
at the end of that long winter,
bullfrogs came out of nowhere,
found our pond and sat fat and horny,
singing.
I could not walk out in the dark
for fear of treading their several leaf shades
into the mud.

Strange, this house,
after years in another loved place
where I could find its bones and warm pulse
blindfolded.
Now my dreams flood with the desperation of frogs,
careless for lust.

I Don't Know Why

Only god or his grandmother
could love him the way he wants to be loved.
As for me, love sits
fly and spider in my chest.
Not enough he says, I must pay:
pulls open wide lips, slips
in the bird, a small one, its breast
feathers and forked tail
snapped over, pushed down, shoved
between teeth, over tongue, stuffed,
then swallowed, warm as a lover.

After the bird, the spider, the fly,
I got the idea, knew the score.
I accepted, ate more, loved less,
wondered why I stayed.
I gave up hope and gentleness;
the pain became hard to ignore.
My ageing and inertia were paid
in bitterness, after dinner chocolates,
a freezer full of cuts of the best.
I lie beside him sick of the mess.
Perhaps I'll die.

Running Away

Caradoc Coaches day-trip *trap trip trap* over the bridge
to Llanbister to Llyn Gwynant
bridges of devils and the coach *put put*
it goes
so slow slow as
red kites whooshing the wind
to the water
to dip
like the road to elsewhere

where I might step from the green bus
and wander off past the shelter's red-painted
Caitlin Price is a Slut!
to climb up past the peckled rocks there
and as the bus dreeps to the distance

take off my shoes to press my bare feet
my head to the sheep-bitten grass
so tight it is so pillow soft
and sleep

On Sleeping Alone

oh my oh my what big teeth you have you letters of love smelling
of sandalwood in your special box of disappointment and raging
not sleeping soundly remembering that you should be the start of
the happy-ever-after story not the little girl swallowed whole to be
saved by the woodman and his wielded axe

what wolves in sheep's clothing

what grannies' bonnets tied with a ribbon under their sweet
    little chins

now I sit tight on the lid

Pandora was not heavy in her hips like me not grounded by her
    own strong living days and nights

I am drawn instead to my own songs to let them sing in the fresh
air love letters to myself wearing the blue slip with the butterflies
I take up the pretty teapot for one the scratchy pen the days the
life floating lonely happy and sad

the blank sheets

Aldi

Twenty years in this town
where I brought up babies,
ate in the cafés,
worked on the till in Tesco.

Now, I slip through its streets,
avoid eye contact. These days
I go to Aldi, even though the kids
won't eat the cereal.
The aisles are empty,
no Rose here or Tina with the belly laugh
and the dirty jokes
and the *So how's married life treating you?*

And although I know which steps
spring will take – snowdrops and lambs,
daffodils, some unexpected sun on a wet hillside,
Creme Eggs by the tills –
I no longer trust even this.

This, after all, is Aldi.
And it has something to do
with what you did to me.

Chicken

I had a strange husband once.
Four years, long enough for it to hurt me badly,
so I could roll up my shirt
and have the scars to show.

We heal more slowly as we age,
don't quite recover our old selves –
falter at the edge of pavements,
not even sure anymore
that we want to cross the road.

Fridge Magnets

Middle aged women
who have had some pain in their lives
are very wise. They kindly come over
with cakes and cards and fridge magnets
with wisdom written thereon:

A Woman Is Like A Teabag,
Stronger In Hot Water, or some such stuff.

Now, my fridge magnet collection
covers the whole of the fridge.

The big wisdom, they say, the hard one, is:
You Must Live In The Present,
Launch Yourself On Every Wave,
Find Eternity In Every Moment.

Can't they see that I am?
I shout it so they can hear it.
I *Don't Cry Because It's Over*,
I *Smile Because It Happened*.

Now I am ready.

They shake their heads, wrap scarves over their hair
like widows at wakes, and leave.
I think that they will come back again.

When You're Ready, The Right Man Will Come Along

Taking my cup of tea back to bed this morning,
the air was still,
but I could just see, obliquely,
the telegraph wire stretched across the street
vibrating and sagging
quite alarmingly.

What bloody heavy sodding bird is that? I wondered.
And just as I thought it
there came into view
a man, all slim and toes all pointy,
pole all shaky,
slinking along, shoulders broad
and fine, strong thighs
pinging and stretching like the wire.

He caught my eye and grinned.
I nodded, but didn't want to distract him,
so slid beneath the covers.

When I came up for air, he had gone.
Later, taking my re-usable bag to the Co-Op,
I found green sequins scattered in the street.

Cattle Lorry Lover

You meet me in the lay-by by Ludlow
on the A49. Is it my heart
or the restlessness of the cattle,
stomping and steaming piss in the back?

You kiss my breasts,
sucking at the nipples,
whilst calves from their mothers
are forced to wait

for my breathing to calm.
Their eyes startle and I climb down,
get back into my Volvo estate.
They sway away
and my breasts' milk drips.

Getting It

To start with, I tried sex with a space hopper:
rolled it around in the corner of my bedroom
while it smiled its dirty smile
and looked like it might help,
but not quite.

I tried sex with an old friend,
safe on the sofa; I felt something
like tracing the lines
on my own palm, sweet dead ends.
Avoided him spending the night.

I tried safe sex with soft swingers,
rubbed against the Hitler moustaches
of middle-class women,
drank tea in the intermission
in Llandrindod Wells hotels.

Alone now in my bed,
I hear a peal of bells, on and on, a joy in my head.
My search flies from hands
outstretched.

I Am My Own Parent

I love my red shoes;
all of the shoes I have loved,
they are.

I swing my legs against the wall,
scuffing them slightly.
My dad is not here to pick them up

by the scruffs of their dirty necks
and leave them shining in the morning.
And now, the arc of my swing

is not quite so high,
the shoes every day a little duller.
At night I leave them in the hall like hope.

In the morning,
absentmindedly dreaming of old loves
and reading poetry until it hurts,

I spring suddenly out of bed
and decide to roll up my life into a fist,
smelling of patchouli and roses, and then

unroll it. And to my surprise,
it becomes a snail's yellow shell, unravelling.
On and on it goes. It's gorgeous.

I tap tap my red shoes
to find I'm already home.

Pink Pyjama Suit

Five, I must have been,
just five, in my pink shiny
shalwar kameez.

Auntie and Karachi pinched my cheeks:
Chorti pyara, little darling,
like a doll,
like a little blonde doll.
Walk this way, try some dancing.
Behen! Now you have your little blonde doll
to play with!

Mummi-ji, I don't want to wear it to school.
North London laughs too easily,
makes fools of us and this mix-up family, this
half-caste council-estate bastard.

Miss Minchin, one arm shorter than the other,
knew how North London could laugh and said:
Knock on all six doors and tell them
Miss Minchin says I must show the children
my clothes from Pakistan.

Mummi-ji, the glass on the doors is too high
and all those eyes
as I turn round and round, up on teachers' tables,
a little blonde doll,
to twist in my pretty pink pyjama suit.

My Mother Moves Into Adolescence

My mother comes round with my star signs,
a thin apple pie, shop-bought,
that no-one will want, and the Daily Mail.
We say thank you.
The boys kiss her and go upstairs.

She presents me with six things:

1.

*You must sort out breakdown for my car Debbie
because my English is bad.*
I get the leaflet, circle the right policy, hand it back to her.

2.

Where must I buy new front door?
I say B&Q? Homebase? I said that before, Mum.
She waits for me to offer to measure it and take her.
I put the kettle on.

3.

Where do I find man to fit new door?
I tell her I don't know, Mum,
look in the Yellow Pages?
She waits for me to get the Yellow Pages.
I get her a piece of cake with her tea.
Just a thin piece... chorti... chorti.
She eats a large piece, noisily.

4.

Where do I find man to fit carpet?
The Yellow Pages, Mum?
Where do I look under?
Carpet Fitters, Mum.

5.

You must show me where to write email to Aleem.
I show her.

6.

I need you write letter to estate agent.
I can't do it today, Mum.
You are so lazy Debbie! she screams.
All her rage spits out.
She throws her mug into the sink and it shatters there.

I liked that green mug with the spots,
from Woolworths.
There is no more Woolworths.
Suddenly,
terribly, unbearably sad
that there is no Woolworths,
I tell her to go and never come back.

My Brown-Eyed Girl

This winter, in our forties,
chatting over the washing up,
my sister and I discovered
that she'd always coveted
my grey green eyes
and I, hers of golden brown,
and *Don't It Make My Brown Eyes*
was never personal enough.

So we swapped, we popped out
our eyeballs, slipped them
into our mouths to moisten them
before slotting into familial sockets.
Then we sat down with a nice pot of tea,
lemon drizzle cake
and little chance of rejection.

The story was in *Chat, The News of the World*
and everywhere we looked.
And now I can see
Crystal Gale sings to me
and Van Morrison never stops.

He Sees Me

I like this man who,
charmed by me,
slips alongside and inside of me
like the tongue of a dog
lapping at my life.

He says,
he says I rise up like a hundred balloons
loosed from a child's hand,
beautiful, bold, even when out of sight.

He says when I sleep I sigh
and he watches me wake and smiles
at the fuzz of my mind and my hair in the morning.

He is charmed, he is charmed; I begin
to charm even myself,
he sees me so lovely.

Quaker Hat

All the women wanted to tip up
his big broad black felt Quaker hat,
as he sat, reasonable, calm, a thinking man;
so too his hat sat, sorted and straight,

and he said *Look!*
Let's ignore my straight hat, the straight straight lines
of me, my hat,
and oh you have a tangle here,
your hat is tangled in your hair,
you will need me to straighten and straighten.

So they looked over there, those women, away
and at *her* hat, her bird's nest hat,
and when it blew off in high winds
she was driven mad by his straight,
big broad black felt Quaker hat,
still sat straight,
and would try to knock it off,
tip it off.

But there were tacks.
That hat was tacked to his head.

Lift Him Up Out

He was always drawn to this kind of woman,
the kind who would survive a nuclear exchange;

the kind who, he felt, would lift him up out
of the wreckage of the car crash by his cock

and his pinched nipples, his body arched up
and greedy for her mouth; the kind of woman

who, on his deathbed, would say something
to take his mind off it, to give him something

(even as the breath gave up)
to live for.

She describes herself like this

I still choose the window seat on buses, trains and planes
and though for now all I can see
is my own reflection
in the glass, in the fading light,
sometimes I can see beyond it.

I am a mother, a field, a house.
Without me, windows darken,
no-one else knows how to put on lights
just to bring the house to life.

I am each of the processes of laundry,
but most of all, the unfolding in winter
of sheets, a sudden punch
of trapped summer on white linen, heat.

I have had many lovers
and I have been many times loved.

When I come I cry out,
and I am the sound of the wind in the trees
and I am the rain on the roof when in love,
or falling.

Small Rain

I fall asleep easily these days.
Life's salt and light back through the years
shortens and lengthens, projects
especially shadows, and I imagine myself

a 1950s baby, overwrapped in a perambulator
with a bouncing chassis, in an autumn garden,
a muffler, a plaid blanket, a shawl
of crochet squares of red and orange and brown.

A passing of clouds over the sun
sends a chill to my fingertips, over-peeping the blanket,
grasping and curled. I imagine my 1950s mother
breathing Craven A smoke through her nose,

red-tipped second finger taking the tobacco grain
from her tongue, feeling small rain and judging
just how damp from the slow flap of the washing
and the red apple-flush of sleep in my cheeks,

just how long.

True Tales of the Countryside

1.

Cheryl can't stand it any longer,
the ewes calling for the lambs.

All day was bad enough, but moving
on the edges of sleep she counts the bleats,

frantic, the milk twitching at teats.
She can feel it, needing the pull and pull,

the milk's steady pulse beating,
mild woolly agony on and on, until

almost silent, but for one mother – it would be her –
never giving up, running back and forth

through the hedge gaps. Searching,
wild as a wolf howling for the moon.

The double glazing cannot shut it out.
Too raw-skinned on council estate gravel,

Cheryl turns her face from the moles'
fly-blown purses strung along the fence.

Tells him she wants to go home.

2.

I picked her up on the way to see my boyfriend,
partly for company and partly to show him how
unexpected I could be, to intrigue him.
She looked harmless, a hippy,
Greenpeace bag, naive city eyes.
It was raining, she was grateful,
even though I could only take her part of the way.
Sorry I have to call in
and get my bloke from work, I said.
She didn't mind – we got on really well;
I could see me in her a bit,
twenty years ago, before babies, divorce,
Guardian Soulmates, other shit.

The trouble was my boyfriend –
a health and safety officer,
today working at the abattoir in Rhayader –
got into the car stepping out of the shiny red puddles,
smelling strongly of beef,
turning to smile at her,
blood splashes
on his white collar
teeth.

3.

Little boy, do not throw your chewing gum
out of the car window
into the verge –
a mouse baby will come smelling the juicy fruits
thinking it better than autumn blackberries
and, feasting greedy as hedgehog gorging,
will choke and die,
its mother stretching and pulling at the sweet mess,
never ever ridding her sleek brown body
of the memory.

4.

This country kid in my class
used to take down the soft pelts
from the farmers' fences,
cut off their little heads
and thread them on strings to dry.

Then, with mother-of-pearl tweezers
and some fine silk, he'd make zips
from the teeth, a long mole smile he would stitch
into mole skin pencil cases.

Sometimes, as a good luck charm,
there'd be a head, a little dead mole head,
toothless, dangling.

The heat in the classroom that summer
and the smell of the poems in the pencil.

Acknowledgements

The BBC programme featuring Germaine Greer, which is referenced in Helen Ivory's introduction, was Balderdash & Piffle, first aired in 2006.

'I put a pen in my cunt once' was first published in *Hallelujah for 50ft Women* (Bloodaxe, 2015).

'On Sleeping Alone' was first published on the website Ink, Sweat and Tears in 2012.

'I Don't Know Why' was first published in *Under the Radar* (Nine Arches Press, 2012).

'My Mother Moves Into Adolescence' was first published in *The Emma Press Anthology of Motherhood* (Emma Press, 2014).

'He Sees Me' was first published in *Hallelujah for 50ft Women* (Bloodaxe, 2015).

'My Brown-Eyed Girl' was first published in the 2015 *Wenlock Poetry Festival Anthology* (Fair Acre Press).

About the poet

Deborah Alma was born in North London. She has an MA in Creative Writing from Keele University, teaches at the University of Worcester and works with people with dementia and at the end of their lives using poetry. She teaches creative writing and is also Emergency Poet in her 1970s ambulance. She is the editor of *The Emergency Poet: An Anti-Stress Poetry Anthology* (Michael O'Mara Books, 2015). She is half-Indian and lives in Powys.

The Emma Press

small press, big dreams

The Emma Press is an independent publisher dedicated to producing beautiful, thought-provoking books. It was founded in 2012 by Emma Wright in Winnersh, UK, and is now based in Birmingham. In 2014 the Emma Press was shortlisted for the Michael Marks Award for poetry pamphlet publishers.

In July-November 2015 we are travelling around the country with 'Myths and Monsters', a tour of poetry readings and workshops aimed at children aged 9-12. This has been made possible with a grant from Grants for the Arts, supported using public funding by the National Lottery through Arts Council England.

Our current publishing programme features a mixture of themed poetry anthologies and single-author poetry and prose pamphlets, with an ongoing engagement with the works of the Roman poet Ovid. We publish books which excite us, and we are often on the lookout for new writing.

Sign up to the monthly Emma Press newsletter to hear about our events, publications and upcoming calls for submissions. All of our books are available to buy from our online shop, as well as to order or buy from all good bookshops.

http://theemmapress.com
http://emmavalleypress.blogspot.co.uk/

Other Emma Press Pamphlets

RASPBERRIES FOR THE FERRY, *by Andrew Wynn Owen*

ISBN: 978 0 9574596 5 6 – PRICE: £6.50

Andrew Wynn Owen dazzles in his debut pamphlet, whisking the reader up with his infectious rhythms and lively sensuality.

IKHDA, BY IKHDA, *by Ikhda Ayuning Maharsi*

ISBN: 978 0 9574596 6 3 – PRICE: £6.50

Reading this book is like being splashed with freezing water and showered with popping candy and wild roses.

OILS, *by Stephen Sexton*

ISBN: 978 1 910139 03 5 – PRICE: £6.50

Belfast poet Stephen Sexton evokes melancholy and a strange kind of romance throughout his brilliant debut pamphlet.

RIVERS WANTED, *by Rachel Piercey*

ISBN: 978 1 910139 04 2 – PRICE: £6.50

Rachel Piercey charms and disturbs in this beautiful, frequently heart-breaking collection of poems about love, identity and home.

MYRTLE, *by Ruth Wiggins*

ISBN: 978 1 910139 12 7 – PRICE: £6.50

Ruth Wiggins celebrates the primal forces of nature and the human heart in her heady debut, which is full of dry humour and wisdom.